Muskwa-Kechika

THE WILD HEART OF CANADA'S NORTHERN ROCKIES

Dedicated to the citizens of the North who participated in the Fort St. John, Fort Nelson and Mackenzie Land and Resource Management Plans, who found common ground, and who made the Muskwa-Kechika a reality.

To Amelia & Jessica —

With the hope that one day you will see these sights & work to protect them!

Muskwa-Kechika

East Tuchodi Lake.

THE WILD HEART OF CANADA'S NORTHERN ROCKIES   BY WAYNE SAWCHUK

Photography and text copyright © 2004 by Wayne Sawchuk

All rights reserved. No part of this publication may be reproduced or transmitted in any form or by any means, electronic or mechanical, including photocopy, recording or any information storage and retrieval system, without prior written permission from the publisher.

Published in Canada by Wayne Sawchuk
Northern Images
Box 1876, Chetwynd, British Columbia, Canada V0C 1J0
ph: 250-788-7871
email: wsawchuk@pris.ca
www.m-k.ca

Produced by Donald A. Pettit
Peace photoGraphics
Box 823, Dawson Creek, British Columbia, Canada V1G 4H8
ph: 1-866-373-8488
email: info@peacephotographics.com
www.peacephotographics.com

National Library of Canada Cataloguing in Publication Data

Sawchuk, Wayne, 1955-
     Muskwa-Kechika : the wild heart of Canada's Northern Rockies / photography and text, Wayne Sawchuk; illustrations and copy editing by Barbara Swail.

"Dedicated to the people who participated in the land and resource management plans, who found common ground and who made the Muskwa-Kechika a reality."
ISBN 0-9687363-5-1

     1. Muskwa-Kechika Management Area (B.C.)--Pictorial works.
2. Muskwa-Kechika Management Area (B.C.) I. Title.

FC3845.M88S28 2004   917.11'87   C2004-900026-8

Design by Denis & Muntener Advertising, Prince George, British Columbia.
Layout by Jesh de Rox.
Illustrations and copy editing by Barbara Swail.
Proof reading by Cees van de Mond.
The Vision of the Muskwa-Kechika Advisory Board, page 20, can be found at www.muskwa-kechika.com.
Cartographic support by Yellowstone to Yukon Conservation Initiative, the B.C. Ministry of Water, Land and Air Protection and Rick Tingey.
Printed and bound in Canada by Friesens.
Printed with vegetable-based inks on paper containing 10 per cent post consumer waste.

Your comments are welcome. Enlargements of these images and information about the sale and distribution of this book are available by contacting Wayne Sawchuk or Peace photoGraphics.

The sale of this book will assist in the conservation of the wilderness and wildlife of the Muskwa-Kechika Management Area.

The Muskwa-Kechika Management Area owes its existence to the efforts of many fine individuals:

To George Smith, National Conservation Director for the Canadian Parks and Wilderness Society – who brought intelligence, persistence and humour to the Northern Rockies campaign, and without whom there would not be a Muskwa-Kechika Management Area.

To Bert Brink of the Federation of B.C. Naturalists and Leo Rutledge, who have carried the vision of protecting the Northern Rockies for many decades, and who have been an inspiration to us all.

To Harvey Locke and Wendy Francis, for their vision of providing the Muskwa-Kechika with the larger context of the Yellowstone to Yukon Conservation Initiative.

To the groups and organizations who supported the Northern Rockies campaign: Alpine Club of Canada, B.C. Environmental Network: Parks and Wilderness Caucus, Federation of B.C. Naturalists Foundation, B.C. Spaces for Nature, B.C. Trappers Association, B.C. Wild, B.C. Wildlife Federation, Canadian Parks and Wilderness Society, Chetwynd Environmental Society, Fort Ware Kaska Dene First Nation, Friends of the Northern Rockies, McLean Foundation, Northern B.C. Guides Association, North Eastern B.C. Wildlife Committee, North Peace Nature Club, North Peace Rod & Gun Club, Our Forests Forever, Outdoor Recreation Council of B.C., Patagonia Inc., Sierra Club of B.C., Western Canada Wilderness Committee and the World Wildlife Fund.

To Vicky Husband, Ric Careless, John Broadhead, Lloyd Manchester, Greg McDade and Colleen McCrory, for both their personal support and that of B.C. Wild, which allowed me to give up logging to support my environmental habit.

To the Brainerd Foundation, Bullitt Foundation, Endswell Foundation, Henry P. Kendall Foundation, Lazar Foundation, Lichen Foundation, McLean Foundation, Sierra Club of B.C. Foundation, Tides Canada Foundation, Vancouver Foundation and the Wilburforce Foundation, who have generously supported my work and the creation of the Muskwa-Kechika.

To the Chetwynd Environmental Society and the B.C. Chapter of the Canadian Parks and Wilderness Society, who have provided invaluable support and encouragement throughout the creation of the Muskwa-Kechika.

To Wayne Soper, both for his personal support and for encouraging the corporate support of Westcoast Energy (now Duke Energy) at critical times in the process.

To Rob McManus, who was instrumental in ensuring the Canadian Association of Petroleum Producers (CAPP) was part of the consensus that created the Muskwa-Kechika.

To Bill Lux, Dave Porter, Dennis Porter and Peter Stone, for the support of the Kaska Dena.

To the government staff who have been involved, just some of whom are: Andy Ackerman, Ray Dimarchi, Gordon Goodman, Warren Mitchell, Derek Thompson, Jim Walker, and the chairs of the LRMPs: Allan Blair, Jim Little, Mary Viszlai-Beale, Jamie Pardy, and Gail Ross.

To Ross Peck, chair of the Muskwa-Kechika Advisory Board, and the Muskwa-Kechika Advisory Board members, who give of themselves for the benefit of all.

To the many who helped in the preparation of this book, some of whom are: Rod Backmeyer, Brian Churchill, Barry Holland, Sandra Kinsey, Bob Peart, Tom Perry, Larry Pynn, Reed Radley, George Smith, Dave Wiens and Liz Williams.

To the great photographers who have been an inspiration to me: Daryl Benson, Raymond Gehman, Patrick Morrow, Graham Osborne, Jerry Pavia and Don Pettit.

To the excellent staff at Peace photoGraphics who have produced this book, particularly Jesh de Rox, layout and graphics wizard; Barbara Swail, eagle-eyed editor and illustrator; Cees van de Mond for skilled and tireless proof reading; and a special thanks to Don Pettit, producer, without whose intellect, professionalism and steadfast pursuit of excellence this book would have been much inferior, if in existence at all.

To my parents, who have fostered my interest in wilderness: my father, Mike, who has fueled my curiosity, independence and persistence, and my mother, Freda, who has taught me respect for the fellow beings in this world, both human and animal – and so much more.

And finally, to my life partner Marce Fofonoff, who has supported the Muskwa-Kechika in countless ways, just a few of which are: editing, proofing, corralling finances, saddling horses, cooking over a lot of smoky campfires, keeping the home fires burning, and providing sage advice and assistance, without which it would have been impossible for me to produce this book, or to pursue the Muskwa-Kechika.

Contents

Preface 8

Introduction 12

History 14

Vision 20

How it Works 22

First Nations 30

The Living Wilderness 36

Eastern Slopes 64

Peace-Finlay 88

Kechika-Liard 104

The Future 134

Photographer's Notes 140

"... the survival of one of the most important wildlife and wilderness complexes in North America hangs in the balance ..."

PREFACE

I first explored B.C.'s Northern Rockies from the back of a horse on an 85-day, two-person, six-horse and one-dog expedition in the summer of 1984. During that trip to the heads of the Prophet, Tuchodi and Muskwa rivers, it was rare to meet another person. We encountered no year-round settlements or human habitation, something that is not unusual. Except for the Alaska Highway corridor, very few people live within the Muskwa-Kechika. This is true wilderness.

Since that first journey, I have snowshoed, hiked and ridden many hundreds of miles through these wild mountains. Out on the trapline on a night as black as pitch, the temperature –20 C (–30 F), I have set my boots, socks and pants on the ice, then eased into the knee deep water of an icy stream to heave a sunken snowmobile onto the bank. The sounds of avalanches and of moose calling and feeding in the cool grey dawn, the soul-touching howl of a wolf pack, and the myriad tiny sounds of the wilderness have wakened me to greet the dawn from one end of the Muskwa-Kechika to the other. Over the years, the spirit of this great land and the wild heart of these rugged mountains have been instilled deep within me.

This book chronicles a few of these experiences, and the selected photographs showcase some of the history, the processes, the animals, the landscapes and the First Nations' values that make up the Muskwa-Kechika.

Many others know what I know – the Muskwa-Kechika is one of the few remaining places in the entire world where a fully-functioning wilderness ecosystem of this complexity and value still lives and breathes as it always has. This knowledge fueled the years of nose-to-nose negotiating that led to the hard-won creation of the Muskwa-Kechika Management Area.

The Muskwa-Kechika Management Area is now at a critical point. Much has been done and all sectors have demonstrated genuine willingness to work together. However, the potential of the Muskwa-Kechika is yet unproven, and there are trouble signs for the future.

It comes down to this: can we seize this opportunity, in this one place, to protect and sustain natural values of global significance, now and forever? Or will the Muskwa-Kechika become a failed experiment in land use planning? I fervently believe we can and will work together to sustain this legacy for generations of both humans and animals. Only time will tell if this optimism is justified. In the meantime, the survival of one of the most important wildlife and wilderness complexes in North America hangs in the balance.

Wayne Sawchuk,
Moberly Lake, B.C.
January 1, 2004.

Previous page: Wolf and Stone's sheep tracks.
Right: Besa River.

The Muskwa-Kechika encompasses a fully functioning, intact predator-prey system, rare in the world today.

Left: A bull moose pauses from the rigours of the rut; a picture of confidence and tranquility.

Below: A female grizzly bear is the epitome of strength.

Introduction

This book reveals one of the most remote and beautiful areas of the world, a vast and primal remnant of the great wilderness that once existed. It also tells the story of divergent interests finding common ground and creating a plan to protect that uncommon wilderness forever.

An inventory of the Muskwa-Kechika inspires awe: 50 intact watersheds, each larger than 5,000 ha (12,400 acres); one of the largest wilderness areas in North America south of the 60th parallel, fully 6.3 million ha (16 million acres) in size; the longest remaining unroaded stretch of the Rocky Mountain Trench, and large pristine chunks of the Cassiar Mountains and Canada's Northern Rockies. Located in north central British Columbia, it is home to a full suite of wildlife species, including most of the world's population of Stone's sheep. It is the traditional home and hunting ground of several First Nations. And it is rich in the natural resources that support our modern lifestyle.

In the Muskwa-Kechika, some hunt for moose, others for oil and gas; some trap, guide and fish, others drill, mine and log. How can delicate ecosystems, wilderness values and resource industries co-exist? The Muskwa-Kechika model demonstrates that, even when self interest brings people together, compromise and consensus can be found. It may also demonstrate a totally new kind of conservation that can sustain both wilderness and the economy, if the model is given the chance to prove itself.

This is the story of nature and human nature, and how, on common ground, the uncommon can happen.

The tufa mound of the Prophet River Hot Springs, laced with animal trails. The warm waters carry minerals that create a lick for many wildlife species.

> *" . . . small dark flakes of chert, smooth on one side, sharp on the edges . . . the ancient hunter chose this campsite for the same reasons we did . . . "*

Remnants of stone age tool making, chert flakes (small blue flakes in the foreground), show on the surface, as Reed Radley and Andy Kadziolka relax at the end of the day.

HISTORY

We pull into the tiny clearing in the buck brush high on the Prophet-Muskwa divide just as the long shadows of evening stretch across the valley. A thick fog begins to form as we tie the horses. Unpacking Big Dan, I notice a shallow hole in the moss beneath his hooves. A bull moose in rut gouged it out, urinated, then rubbed his shoulders in the mixture, creating the equivalent of pungent moose aftershave. But also there, out of place in the bottom of the moose hole, are tiny chips of stone, small dark flakes of chert, smooth on one side, sharp on the edges. Warmed by a campfire like ours, an ancestor, one of the first peoples, flaked stone tools here. The ancient hunter chose this campsite for the same reasons we did: dry mossy ground, firewood close at hand, balsam thickets for shelter, and a clear view across the valley to nearby mountains. How long ago? Centuries? Millennia?

It may have been 20,000, even 30,000 years ago, when the first nomads reached this continent. If they came over the Bering land bridge, they then traveled south along an ice-free corridor that ran parallel to the eastern slopes of the Rocky Mountains at the western edge of the great plains, at that time covered by mile-deep sheets of ice. This corridor led down the length of the mountains: far enough east to avoid the nearly impassable Rocky Mountain spine and far enough west to miss the dangerous crossings of the major rivers issuing from the flanks of the mountains. On dry ridges and the lowest passes, this ancient travel route can sometimes be found today, at times a faint depression in the moss, nearly impossible to find in some places

Above, left to right: Wayne Sawchuk and George Smith with the "Northern Rockies – Totally Wild" campaign poster that assisted the genesis of the Muskwa-Kechika. The poster listed 22 supporting organizations, ranging from the B.C. Trappers Association to the Federation of B.C. Naturalists.

Wendy Francis, of the Yellowstone to Yukon Conservation Initiative, contemplates a teepee frame still standing near the Muskwa River in 2003.

The historic, and pre-historic, Davie Trail heads south up the Kechika River and the Rocky Mountain Trench.

Fort St. John Land and Resource Management Planning table representatives at Crying Girl Prairie at a 1994 planning meeting. The Fort St. John Plan was one of three that created the Muskwa-Kechika.

and missing entirely in others. Along the way, a string of archeological sites, like the isolated flakes at our little camp, bear testament to ancient human presence.

More recent signs of human use are also found: tree blazes, drying racks and grave sites. Leo Rutledge, a long-time guide-outfitter, tells of teepee poles standing by large moose licks on the Prophet River in the 1930s. Even today, on the flats of the Muskwa River, a long-abandoned teepee frame still stands in the forest, a persistent reminder of times gone by.

The Coming of the European

West of the Rockies runs another north-south travel route, following the Rocky Mountain Trench from Lower Post to Fort Ware. The Davie Trail, used by First Nations for eons past, became an alternate route to the Yukon gold fields when it was improved for prospectors by the North West Mounted Police in the 1890s. Old axe-cut, moss-covered stumps and widened sections along steep hillsides are still-visible signs of that long-ago labour.

In the early part of the last century, the winter silence of the Northern Rockies was disturbed only by the soft swish of snowshoes as white and native trappers pursued fur bearers such as beaver, lynx and fisher. Marten, renamed sable for the salons of New York and Paris, was then, as now, the staple fur. If weather, luck and prices held, it was a good living for those who survived. Winter brought weeks of –40 C (–40 F) temperatures and a person might not meet another for the six snowy months of the year. Access was by dog team and snowshoe in the winter months and horse and canoe in the summer. The nearest road was many weeks and hundreds of kilometers to the south.

All this changed abruptly in 1942 when Canada and the United States agreed to build a land route to Alaska in response to the perceived threat of invasion from Japan. The Alcan Highway, now known as the Alaska Highway, was built in just eight months through 2,400 km (1,500 mi.) of uncharted muskeg, dense forest and precipitous mountains – an incredible feat of engineering and human perseverance, and one that would change the lives of northerners forever. For some isolated, largely First Nations villages, the first news of change was the caterpillar tractors that came crashing through the forest. Suddenly, town was just a ride away, and a tidal wave of social change came in by highway.

Today, the Alaska Highway is a major tourist attraction. Some 350,000 travelers from around the world head north each year, lured by the wild and majestic scenery of northeast British Columbia, the Yukon and Alaska. The highway winds through the Muskwa-Kechika for 200 km (120 mi.), offering access to resorts, hiking, fishing and wildlife viewing right from the roadside, or wilderness pack train and fly-in trips for the more adventurous.

Here too can be found some of the most sought-after hunting experiences in North America. Abundant wildlife, thriving in spectacular wilderness settings, supports a multi-million-dollar-a-year guide-outfitting industry, the major source of revenue in the Muskwa-Kechika for over half a century.

Industrial resource extraction follows the highway too. New side roads are pushed into ancient wilderness every year and natural gas, trees and minerals are transported to markets in the south. Change has become the new order of the day, change that may threaten traditional activities, industries and recreational uses that already exist on the land.

A Northerner's Story

When I was a boy, my father and uncles talked about "going up in the mountains" to a fabulous land somewhere "up north." Led by outfitters like Leo Rutledge, with native guides like Marvin Desjarlais and Johnny Gauthier, pack trains of 50 horses took a month to reach the hunting country. The caribou were so thick up there, they said, the bulls would come into camp at night, or charge the pack trains on the trail, and try to gore the horses. I didn't know it then, but the land they were talking about was the Northern Rockies.

The wilderness surrounding our family's farm, 19 km (12 mi.) west of the small town of Chetwynd, was really part of the same great ecosystem. In the late '50s when I was a child, northeastern B.C., and the foothills of the Rockies where we lived, was lightly touched by human hand. The exploitation of natural gas was just beginning and logging was limited to a few small mills scattered in the valley bottoms. The only major road, the Hart Highway, connected the recently-built Alaska Highway in the east to the B.C. interior. All but a few of the remaining valleys were roadless and pristine. Today, almost all of the valleys south of the Peace have been roaded, and their forests fragmented, in the search for timber, natural gas or coal. As a result, many now feel that the future looks bleak for wide-ranging animals like caribou in the landscape south of the Peace River.

I come from a family of loggers, and this was my work for many years. But the wilderness called, and most summers I headed into the mountains with horses. In 1983, short excursions began to give way to major expeditions lasting as long as 85 days. Traversing some of the wildest backcountry in the world, I couldn't escape the jarring contrast between the scarred and roaded industrial landscapes where my family worked, and the wildlife-rich, pristine wilderness I visited in the all too short northern summers.

Then, in the late 1980s, my uncle Norman offered to sell his wilderness trapline on the Gataga River, in the heart of the Northern Rockies. Raised with the stories of Jack London, and my grandmother's tales of trapline life, I leapt at the chance. Once my interest in the logging equipment was sold, I was living the wilderness life I craved. There, the animals became my neighbours. I began to develop a profound respect for the fellow beings that inhabited the wilderness, and an understanding began to grow. Their world was incredibly complex and intricate, to a degree that just might exceed our capacity to understand it. Each piece, no matter how insignificant it might appear, may be, and probably is, important to the whole. Who knows what our activities may be destroying through sheer ignorance alone?

Because I saw and participated in the destruction of wilderness in the place where I grew up, I began to worry that the same thing was going to happen in the north I had come to know and love. It became clear to me that although we need the employment and benefits that come from natural resources like timber, natural gas and minerals, there are some places that are just too valuable to destroy in the relentless "march of progress." One of these places is the Northern Rockies of British Columbia.

The Birth of a Vision: the Creation of the Muskwa-Kechika Management Area

A mapping project conducted by the B.C. Ministry of

Forests in 1992, the Inventory of Undeveloped Watersheds, identified more than 50 adjoining watersheds in northern B.C. that were virtually pristine, each with an area greater than 5,000 ha (12,400 acres). These watersheds are located in the Northern Rockies and Cassiars. Together they make up the largest wilderness area in the province of British Columbia by a wide margin.

Land use issues in northeast B.C. were heating up in the early 1990s. Interest in oil, gas, timber and mineral resources was building rapidly, and recreational use was increasing. I began to feel that the threats to the wilderness shown on the Inventory of Undeveloped Watersheds map could no longer be ignored. I began to pull together like-minded northerners: First Nations, guides, hunters, trappers, naturalists and conservationists. At the same time, George Smith, the National Conservation Director of the Canadian Parks and Wilderness Society, and Kevin Scott, also of CPAWS, initiated a background mapping project of the region. Very quickly, George and I joined forces united by the common passion to preserve this remarkable place.

In 1992, George and I launched the "Northern Rockies – Totally Wild" campaign aimed at protecting the globally important wilderness of northern B.C. It wasn't a new idea. For decades, Bert Brink, of the Federation of B.C. Naturalists, had advocated a park in the Redfern area. Ex-guide-outfitter Leo Rutledge pressed for national park status for the entire eastern slopes, while another pioneer guide-outfitter, Skook Davidson, had done the same for the Kechika drainage to the west. Rich Petersen, of the B.C. Wildlife Federation, had long advocated for protection of wildlife on the eastern slopes. Jim Walker, of the B.C. Wildlife Branch, was working toward the same goals from within government. The "Totally Wild" campaign added to these ideas, and brought together a wide spectrum of interests and organizations, all united by the conviction that protecting the wilderness, the wildlife and the traditional uses of the Northern Rockies was critical.

To support the campaign, my partner Marce Fofonoff and I began to lead horseback expeditions into the mountains. We went to explore, to investigate and finally to introduce a variety of people to the wonders of the Northern Rockies. We have had the privilege of leading our pack string into some of the wildest country on the continent, for expeditions lasting six to 10 weeks each summer, accompanied by scientists, conservationists, media, government and others. The expeditions have been life-changing experiences for many. Rarely has a visitor failed to experience a deep connection with the wildness and the natural world.

Also, in 1992, an elegant solution to increasing land use pressures in B.C. was initiated: let interest groups sort it out themselves via a community and consensus-based, multi-sectoral process that would produce a Land and Resource Management Plan, or LRMP. Each LRMP was mandated to recommend future land use direction, including identifying new parks and protected areas sufficient to satisfy the United Nations Bruntland Commission's recommendation that 12 per cent of the land base should be set aside to maintain biodiversity in the long term. I volunteered to sit on the Fort Nelson, Fort St. John and Mackenzie processes that shared the responsibility for planning the Northern Rockies, (as well as the Dawson Creek LRMP, located to the south of the Northern Rockies) representing the environment conservation sector, and soon I was receiving funding from foundations and supporters to do so. Little did I know that the process would take almost 10 years to complete, and implementation of the plans much longer.

A long list of diverse and often contradictory sectors were invited to each table. For instance, long term, high paying jobs were most important to the labour sector. Access to the land base and wildlife topped the list for hunters and anglers. The forest industry wanted access to the fibre resource and the oil and gas industry wanted access for hydrocarbon exploration. Snowmobilers wanted recreational access. Community representatives wanted a vibrant economy that would generate wealth, employment and stability for the citizens, while the environment and conservation interests wanted to sustain wilderness, wildlife and habitat.

The non-industrial sectors agreed that retaining

wilderness was of primary importance. If habitat was preserved, the animals would remain. And if existing types of access were maintained but not allowed to increase, each user group would continue to enjoy the Northern Rockies as it had in the past.

First Nations chose not to participate, or attended as observers only, citing issues such as potential conflicts with aboriginal or treaty rights, or with future treaty settlements.

As negotiations at the tables proceeded, it soon became clear no sector could have everything it wanted. Then, through the give and take of discussion and debate, unexpected solutions began to emerge. Problems were chewed over, examined, discarded. The parts that worked were kept and in the end, people realized, "Hey, I can live with that!" One after another, seemingly insurmountable problems were solved with creativity and consensus. Adversaries began to develop understanding and respect, even friendships.

Although the process was sometimes difficult, with the tables "locked in cooperation" year after year, each sector realized that the process would go ahead with or without its participation. If consensus was reached, many vexing land use issues would be solved successfully. If consensus wasn't reached, compromise would be imposed by the provincial government. This was a powerful incentive for sectors to bargain in good faith. With the help of remarkable patience and willingness to compromise, and four to seven years of work, each plan was agreed to with total consensus, with the exception of mining interests at two of the tables. This position was consistent with that taken by mining representatives at other planning processes across the province.

Outside of the Northern Rockies, the tables recommended that the land be zoned for high and medium intensity industrial use. To protect special non-industrial values, parks and special management areas were identified.

Each of the three responsible LRMPs agreed that maintaining the wilderness and wildlife of the Northern Rockies was a key priority. To maintain these globally important values each recommended:

- that their portion of the Northern Rockies be legally designated as part of the Muskwa-Kechika Management Area (M-KMA), with the goal of maintaining the wilderness and wildlife forever while allowing sensitive and temporary industrial resource extraction in non-park areas

- that new protected areas and parks be established in the Northern Rockies and that these be included under the new designation

- that an advisory board based on sector representation be set up to oversee the area and that a fund be established to support management activities in the Muskwa-Kechika.

The trade-off at the tables was clear. Outside the Muskwa-Kechika, industrial development would proceed as usual. Parks would be off limits to industrial development and the construction of roads. Inside the Muskwa-Kechika, the stunning natural environment would receive world class management, with all roads and industrial impacts, where allowed, removed entirely at the end of the development cycle.

These monumental and groundbreaking agreements were accepted and approved by the government of the day. They are a powerful source of pride for each person who was part of the consensus of the LRMPs.

The End of a Frontier

The planning process for some was a bittersweet experience. Completed planning means the entire land base is now zoned for management. It is the end of the unknown, the end of wilderness without limit. Together, the people of the north preserved a great northern wilderness, but signed and sealed the end of a frontier.

the Vision

THE VISION OF THE MUSKWA-KECHIKA ADVISORY BOARD

We, the Advisory Board, in partnership with the provincial government, will be stewards of the Muskwa-Kechika Management Area.

We will provide direction and leadership in balancing industrial and other human activity with the sensitive management and protection of a vast and unique natural environment.

We will ensure that the fisheries, wildlife and wilderness values of the M-KMA will be maintained for countless generations.

In working toward this vision, the Advisory Board will promote and encourage effective and innovative resource management methods, based on the highest quality of research. Through research and funding activities, we seek world class management, monitoring, and mitigation to minimize the human footprint.

Through educational and promotional activities, the Advisory Board will raise awareness about the M-KMA's globally significant environmental values, aboriginal and non-native inhabitants, and their cultural histories.

The author's brother, Paul Sawchuk, contemplates the upper Toad River valley on expedition in the Muskwa-Kechika, as the first snows of winter threaten.

*"The Muskwa-Kechika Management Area
was formed in the crucible
of the land use planning processes..."*

Below: Marce Fofonoff, with Jarvis and Bev Wice of the Chetwynd Environmental Society, celebrate after installing a road sign announcing the Muskwa-Kechika boundary at Liard River. The sign includes the Kaska Dena translation of "Have a safe journey."

HOW IT WORKS

Resource Management Zones (RMZs): Balanced Protection and Industrial Use

The Muskwa-Kechika Management Area was formed in the crucible of the land use planning processes that created the Fort St. John, Fort Nelson and Mackenzie Land and Resource Management Plans. The LRMPs recommended a legislated network of Provincial Parks surrounded by Special Management Zones (SMZs) where innovative and environmentally responsible industrial resource use is permitted. In all non-park zones, the land use plans stipulate that wilderness, wildlife and cultural values must be protected while operations take place, and afterwards, the land returned to its previous wilderness state. Named for two of the major rivers within the area, the Muskwa-Kechika Management Area Act enshrines these recommendations in legislation.

The Muskwa-Kechika was designated without prejudice to First Nations' values and interests, and ways to fully accommodate these must be developed in the future. In the interim, traditional First Nations' activities will continue to take place.

Within the Muskwa-Kechika, there are four distinct kinds of Resource Management Zones, each with a separate set of objectives: Provincial Parks and Protected Areas; Special Management Zones; Special: Wildland Zones; and one Enhanced Resource Development Zone.

Provincial Parks and Protected Areas

Scattered throughout the Muskwa-Kechika are 20 provincial parks encompassing 1.6 million ha (four million acres). These provide the highest level of protection for a broad spectrum of values, and encompass areas of pristine wilderness, intact drainages, ice fields, vibrant rivers, lakes and streams, and special features such as animal licks, hot springs or First Nations sites. Some, like Muncho Lake Park and Liard River Hotsprings Park, already existed and were included in the Muskwa-Kechika at the time of its formation. Others, ranging in size from the 180 ha (450 acres) Prophet River Hotsprings Park, to the

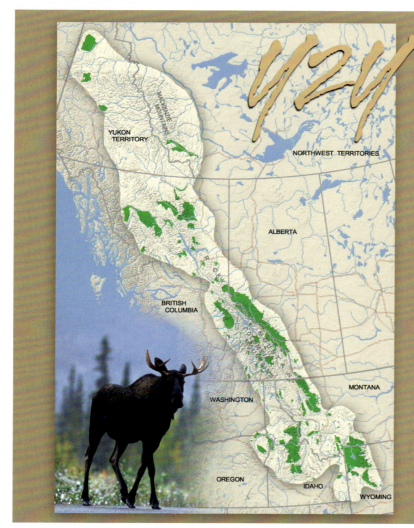

Y2Y Conservation Initiative Study Area

The Muskwa-Kechika encompasses a vast reservoir of healthy animal populations and habitat. While important in its own right as a representation of the vast diversity of life that once existed across the North American continent, the M-K is important on a broader level. It constitutes a significant portion of a corridor of life that stretches along the mountains between Yellowstone Park in Wyoming State and the Yukon Territory. The M-K is a reservoir of genetic diversity that will re-supply the entire corridor, provided that animals are able to travel north and south as they always have.

The Yellowstone to Yukon Conservation Initiative seeks to ensure that existing habitat connections throughout the entire Rocky Mountain chain remain healthy, from Yellowstone to Yukon, and that connections are repaired where they have been severed. By helping to keep the natural heritage of the Rocky Mountains healthy, the Y2Y Initiative will protect not only wildlife, but also the human communities and economies that are part of this great landscape.

665,700 ha (1.64 million acres) Northern Rocky Mountains Park, were designated after years of negotiation and compromise. All parks are off limits to logging, mining, hydroelectric generation, and oil and gas extraction. Road building for any reason is not allowed. Recreational activities such as hunting, angling, hiking, horseback riding, snowmobiling and jetboating, as well as commercial guiding and trapping, can take place if they do not compromise environmental integrity.

Non-Park Resource Management Zones

The remaining Special Management Zones, Special: Wildland Zones and one Enhanced Resource Development Zone encompass some 4.7 million ha (11.6 million acres). Wilderness values can be as high or higher than those in adjacent parks, but these zones often have significant industrial resource values as well. The land use planning tables worked long and hard to find ways to enable resource extraction while maintaining important natural values, and these zones are the areas of greatest compromise.

Special Management Zones

In the Special Management Zones, all new roads and industrial development must be removed and reclaimed at the end of the development cycle. An exception occurs in the Fox and Obo SMZs. Because of high timber values and significant First Nations interest in accessing these resources, as well as potential mineral values, primary roads needed for timber production are allowed to remain in place. No new public motorized recreational access will be allowed before or after operations have begun. The requirements to reclaim roads and remove infrastructure may mean higher costs, but the Muskwa-Kechika's SMZs may repay that expense by fostering the development of new technologies that will be lighter on the land. These techniques will also help to create the social license that industry needs to operate in these exceedingly sensitive areas.

Special: Wildland Zones

These zones are located on the western side of the Muskwa-Kechika and have very high wilderness values. Natural gas and mineral extraction are allowed but, because of difficult road building terrain, high wilderness values and low timber values, these zones are exempt from timber harvesting. All roads must be temporary.

Facing page and above, left to right: Recreation in the Muskwa-Kechika.

An all terrain vehicle (ATV) sets off on a designated route.

Terminus Mountain Wilderness Adventures' lodge on the Kechika River.

River boats offer access on the major rivers, including the Muskwa and the Kechika.

Guide-outfitting has long been a staple use. Here outfitters Dave Wiens and Ross Peck glass for animals.

Guides Kenny Napoleon and Eddy Calliou cinch the 'diamond hitch.'

Eco-tourism and horseback trips are an exciting experience. Mary Martin and husband Bob Peart 'learn' about horses.

Journalist Priscilla Phillips on expedition in the high country, gathering first-hand material for a B.C. Outdoors Magazine article.

Enhanced Resource Development Zone

To accommodate an expanding volume of visitor traffic and related services already there, the Alaska Highway corridor has been designated as an Enhanced Resource Management Zone. Most visitors to the Muskwa-Kechika come via this corridor.

The Muskwa-Kechika Advisory Board

The Muskwa-Kechika Management Area Act requires an advisory board to advise on natural resource management. An important goal is to ensure that the legislated mandate to "maintain in perpetuity the wilderness quality, and the diversity and abundance of wildlife and the ecosystems on which it depends while allowing resource development and use in parts of the Muskwa-Kechika Management Area designated for those purposes" is upheld.

The board reflects the diversity of interests that created the land use plans, including the forestry, mining, and oil and gas industries, recreational users, organized labour, local governments, guide-outfitters and trappers, local and provincial environment and conservation interests, non-commercial hunters and anglers, and First Nations. This wide range of potentially competitive interests requires participants to use the consensus method of decision making. Most participants find consensus far preferable to

majority rule because the interests of all, not just those with the winning vote, are represented in the final solution.

Given that the Muskwa-Kechika covers more than 6.6 per cent of British Columbia, the cost of running the board is a small price to pay for the management certainty that results.

Resource Planning

If wilderness and wildlife are to be protected, human activities on the land must be carefully planned to minimize impact. The Muskwa-Kechika Management Area Act requires that oil and gas pre-tenure plans, park master plans, recreation management plans, wildlife management plans and landscape unit objectives for forestry must be in place before new commercial or industrial tenures or licenses are granted. Originally, the act also required that all mining activities occurring off-tenure be subject to joint sign-off by the B.C. Ministry of Environment and the Ministry of Energy and Mines. Changes to the act mean this vital oversight mechanism no longer applies.

Muskwa-Kechika Trust Fund

The act directs the establishment of a trust fund. Originally set at $3 million plus $1 million matching funds annually, the fund has been reduced to $1 million annually, plus an additional $1 million per year available to match funds from other sources. These funds are allocated by government, based on recommendations of the Muskwa-Kechika Advisory Board. The fund has supported wildlife studies, recreation plans, educational programs, clean-up programs, trailhead signage and many other projects.

Facing page and above, left to right: Activities of the Muskwa-Kechika Advisory Board.

The Board meets two to three times each year to assist in the management of the Muskwa-Kechika. The June 2000 Toad River meeting is pictured.

The Muskwa-Kechika Fund supports wildlife monitoring. Here a collared cow and calf caribou cross the Alaska Highway.

Gillian Radcliffe, wildlife researcher, investigates a caribou mortality in Northern Rocky Mountains Park.

Hank Pokiak, contractor, pauses from constructing an ATV trail bridge over the Besa River. Hank fabricated the beams for the bridge in his back yard.

These barrels, containing a range of petroleum products left behind by an unsuccessful mining exploration project, have been removed from a sub-alpine valley and flown to an airstrip for disposal. Abandoning industrial waste is no longer allowed in the Muskwa-Kechika Management Area.

Trailhead signs such as this one at Skook's Landing on the Liard River have been installed at some 18 roadside locations around the Muskwa-Kechika. In the backcountry of the Muskwa-Kechika, trails are left unsigned to maintain a true wilderness experience.

Liz Logan, chief of the Fort Nelson Band, and Ross Peck, Chair of the Muskwa-Kechika Advisory Board, mark Chief Logan's service on the Muskwa-Kechika Advisory Board.

Facing page, bottom: Muskwa-Kechika Advisory Board members and staff at Stone Mountain Safaris lodge at Toad River, June 2000. Board members are identified by 'B.M.' (not all are present.) Left to right, standing: Andy Ackerman, Brian Churchill, Paul Mitchell-Banks, Neil Meagher B.M., Rick Publicover, Bill Lux B.M., Wally Eamer, Dave Porter B.M., Dennis Porter B.M., Bruce McKnight B.M., Julian Griggs, Jack Sime B.M. Seated: Arnica Wills, Dave Wiens, Ellie Wiens, John Cashore – Initial Chair, Lynn Tiedemann, David Stuart B.M., Mavis Brown, Wayne Sawchuk B.M. Kneeling: Warren Mitchell, Bobby Jackson B.M., Karen Goodings B.M., Barry Holland B.M., George Smith B.M., Ross Peck B.M., Jim Stephenson B.M., Mark Tiedemann.

West Tuchodi Lake and the Tuchodi River valley.

First Nations

Still wet from the thighs down, we urge our little pack string across the Keily Creek flats. The blue waters of the Besa River are largely cleansed of glacial silt by Redfern Lake a few miles upstream, but the river is running high and swift and the crossing was a deep one. The year is 1984, and it is our first time into the valley of the Besa. Warmed by the July sun, we ride down a trail on the margin of the meadow. And there, leaning on a small spruce tree is a pole with cross bar – an ancient cross with its ends carved with care.

The history of First Nations' use in the Muskwa-Kechika stretches back into the depths of time, long before this cross was raised, and it continues to the present day. Long before the first white explorers were shown the way through the Northern Rockies by native guides, aboriginal peoples had been living in these mountains, following the trails of moose, caribou and sheep as they hunted. This knowledge was invaluable to the trapping and guide-outfitting industries, and for a century, native peoples have been making a living using the knowledge gathered over the millennia.

Today, many First Nations peoples live in, visit or use the Muskwa-Kechika. On the east live the Treaty 8 First Nations: Blueberry River, Doig River, Fort Nelson, Halfway River, Prophet River, Saulteau and West Moberly. On the west are located the Daylu Dena Council, Dease River First Nation, Kaska Dena Council, Fireside Community, the Kwadacha Band and the Tsay Keh Dene. Today, First Nations continue to carry out traditional activities such as hunting, fishing, berry gathering and the collection of important medicinal plants.

Craig McCook of the Kwadacha Band takes a break from a raft expedition to contemplate a long-abandoned First Nations cabin, used for trapping, on the Gataga River.

Left: William Davis of the Doig River First Nation points out a "Dechinn," a First Nations sacred cross signifying a wildlife sanctuary at Keily Creek.

Right: A First Nations grave at Crying Girl Prairie, on the Graham River. In the early part of the last century, disease decimated a native band, leaving behind one young girl. This grave may be associated with that sad event.

In the future, First Nations will be more and more involved in activities such as natural gas exploration and development, forestry and commercial recreation, both inside and outside the Muskwa-Kechika.

It is critical that both the traditional activities of First Nations, as well as their new and evolving roles, be recognized and accommodated. This means an increasingly significant role for First Nations in the planning and management of the Muskwa-Kechika, something that will only improve and enhance the management of this great area in the future.

When we leave the mountains in the fall of 1984, we hear the story of the cross. The Keily Creek valley has long had great significance for First Nations, because the many salt licks where animals congregate, along with a variety of diverse habitats, create a rich wildlife community in the valley. Legend says that an important chief erected this cross (called a *Dechinn*) as a sign that the valley was always to be left unhunted, except in time of need or famine, so that the people would always have a source of animals, and the animals would always have a refuge.

The vision of the ancient cross maker of the Keily valley seems to grow ever stronger with the passage of time. In a natural world increasingly under threat, it seems the Muskwa-Kechika is that refuge for wildlife, wilderness and the people who depend on wild things, that the old ones dreamed of so long ago.

The Stone-Macdonald family, brother and sisters, live close to the land at Moose Lake, on the Toad River.

Top: Maggie and Walter, Bottom: Elsie and Rose.

Top: A cabin in the village of Fort Ware looks out on the Muskwa-Kechika to the west, north, and east.

Bottom: Charlie Boya, former chief of the Kwadacha Band of Fort Ware, and Miriam, Caroline and Charlotte, members of his family. The Boya family and their pack dogs walked up the Fox River to spend the night with us at Nine-mile, north of Fort Ware in the Rocky Mountain Trench.

Top: Drivers Les McMahon (left) and Tim Brown (right) of the West Moberly Band, with a load of bison meat and children on their ATVs waiting for our pack string to pass in the Sikanni valley.

Bottom left: Charlotte Boya and a pack dog on the trail north of Fort Ware.

Bottom right: George Smith catches a riverboat ride on the Finlay River with a Fort Ware family.

the Living Wilderness

"There's an elk! Look, a bunch, on the hillside!" Liz Williams points across the valley. Below the elk, a mother grizzly and two yearling cubs lift their heads from the lush grass to watch us. The big bear stands with front paws lifted, then drops to all fours, turns, and with cubs in tow, heads off up the mountain and disappears behind a balsam thicket. In the late July heat we are sweating from the climb up from the Prophet River and it's time to call a lunch stop. Up ahead is a patch of shale, and movement. A hundred meters away, four Stone's sheep skitter about, nervously licking the soil. Behind them, two caribou trot down the slope. Gazing out across the valley, enjoying our crackers and kippers, Michael Coon and Pat O'Reilly count elk as we lounge - over 40 dot the green hillsides. "Look! Another bear!" Pat points as a fourth grizzly, larger than the female we have just seen, strides purposefully down the opposite slope toward us.

Like the upper Prophet, much of the Muskwa-Kechika provides a geography and climate ideal for grazing animals. The rainshadow on the east slopes of the Rocky Mountains combines with abundant summer sunlight to create rich grasslands, home to large numbers of Stone's sheep, moose, caribou, elk, deer, mountain goats and, in some areas, bison. These grazing animals are found throughout the Muskwa-Kechika, along with their predators, black

A bull moose in rut stalks ashore after swimming the lake, intent on meeting the cows feeding in the shallows.

A grizzly veers around our camp on the bank of the Gataga River, gazing intently at the horses grazing just down river. Fortunately the horses didn't panic or run, but simply stared back at the bear, who quietly went on his way, digging roots on the sandbars as he left.

bears, wolves and wolverines, and a host of birds, fish, insects, small mammals and furbearers.

The subalpine is heavily used by wildlife in summer. When the deep snows of winter arrive, they descend to their wintering grounds in the lower elevation valleys. It is of critical importance that the animals can move between different types of habitat as they need to. For many species, such as caribou and grizzly, this is only possible in an intact, unfragmented landscape.

Because the Muskwa-Kechika is largely without roads, the fabric of the ecosystem binding these animals to their habitat is still functioning largely as it always has. Thus the whole is greater than the sum of its parts – a fully functioning, intact predator-prey system, rare in the world today. Preserving the continuity of this rare and fragile balance is one of the great challenges, and potential triumphs of the Muskwa-Kechika.

As the elk stare down from the heights, the big grizzly beelines towards us at a steady amble. It is obvious the ecosystem is functioning well in the upper Prophet. But we have no desire to become permanent parts of that ecosystem. With a "Let's go! Let's go!" to the horses, we mount up and set off once again for the Muskwa divide, checking behind us as we travel.

Top left: Soopolallie berries, a favourite food of grizzly bears.

Bottom left: Soopolallie berries after they've been through the bear. First Nations guides call this "pie filling."

Top right: In the spring, sap rises first in the bases of the spruce and balsam trees. Grizzly bears rip the bark from the tree and scrape the fresh cambium layers with their front teeth, leaving long grooves in the wood. Many trees are killed this way, enough so that grizzly-caused tree mortality may be a significant factor limiting the spread of trees into alpine or subalpine areas.

Bottom right: Long claws identify the track of a grizzly.

A caribou calf, half grown in early fall, feeds from its mother. Caribou utilize a "dispersion strategy" to avoid predators; they spread out across the landscape in order to make location by predators difficult. An increase in predator numbers can limit the effectiveness of this strategy. Increasing elk or moose populations will also increase wolf numbers, working against the survival of the caribou. This is an example of a dynamic interrelationship characteristic of complex ecosystems.

Top: A wolf regards the photographer with a wary eye. Wolves are an important predator in the Muskwa-Kechika, and are an indicator of an intact predator prey system.

Bottom left: The tracks of two wolves, one heavier and larger than the other.

Bottom right: All that remains of a caribou eaten by wolves: a chunk of jaw; a scrap of bone; and hair.

Facing page: Aspen bark is eaten by moose in the depths of winter, when snow is deep and browsing difficult. These trees have been scarred repeatedly over the years. Moose do not walk around a tree as they eat, but instead graze from one tree to the next. As a result, larger aspen trees are rarely killed from being used in this way.

Above: Bull moose in July, near the Chisca River. This burnt area is thick with willows that provide rich moose feed. A moose's antlers are among the fastest growing structures in the animal kingdom and are grown and lost each year. This moose appears ready to challenge or charge, even though his antlers are far from full grown.

Left: Fresh moose track.

Facing page: Stone's sheep ewes and lambs feed on the tufa mounds of the Prophet River Hotsprings. The deposits act as a lick, and large numbers of elk, moose, sheep, caribou as well as occasional wolves and grizzly bears visit the area regularly. The lick is the heart of a thriving wildlife system.

Above: Stone's sheep ram, an animal gifted with extraordinary eyesight. Sheep do not lose their horns, which continue growing and increasing in length and size throughout their lifetime.

Elk cows spook and run at a lick on Keily Creek, in Redfern-Keily Park.

A caribou bull, antlers still in velvet, strides along a Prophet River sandbar.

Facing page: Cow and calf caribou swim a northern lake. The hair of a caribou is hollow, and this extra floatation holds the animal high in the water as it swims.

Above: Caribou cows lick minerals and salt on the edge of the Alaska Highway in early October. Caribou cows with calves carry their antlers in velvet into the early fall, and do not drop their antlers until spring. Caribou bulls lose their antlers in early winter, the earliest of all North American deer.

A fisher track shows a thick, bushy tail.

Winter winds have filled moose tracks in deep snow.

The slide-dot-dot-slide of an otter, searching for f

arch wanderlust strikes a porcupine, leaving signs of quills
nd a thick, heavy tail.

The untiring lope of a wolverine.

A varying hare swerves course. Did it see an owl?

Backlit by the setting sun, a beaver swims the quiet waters of a northern lake.

A host of smaller species adds to the richness of the system. The whole is greater than the sum of its parts, and there are a lot of parts in this complex ecosystem.

Top left: A spider web reflects the geometry of the chase.

Bottom left: A white admiral butterfly and three pink-edged sulphur butterflies drink from a muddy game trail.

Top right: To be avoided – the nest of bald faced hornets – large black and white wasps that sting with little provocation.

Bottom right: A wolf spider on the prowl.

Top left: A darner (dragonfly) pauses for a sunny rest.

Bottom left: A shadow reveals a smoky horntail on an alder leaf.

Top right: The elegance of small things – a chipmunk on the search for seeds.

Bottom right: A minnow suspended above its shadow in the shallows.

Facing page: A squirrel midden. The squirrels have gathered spruce cones for winter food. Squirrel middens are spaced 100 to 200 meters (300 to 600 feet) apart throughout the forest. They are visited by all furbearers, and play a small but critical role in the boreal forest.

Top: A red squirrel chatters from a spruce tree.

Bottom left and right: Bastard toadflax is a bright, but tasteless berry, generally not eaten by humans. Yet, one finds the discarded peels along forest trails, the seed eaten by squirrels or other small animals. Even the smallest part of the vast ecosystem in the Muskwa-Kechika contributes to the whole.

The smoke of a forest fire bronzes the reflected light of the sun.

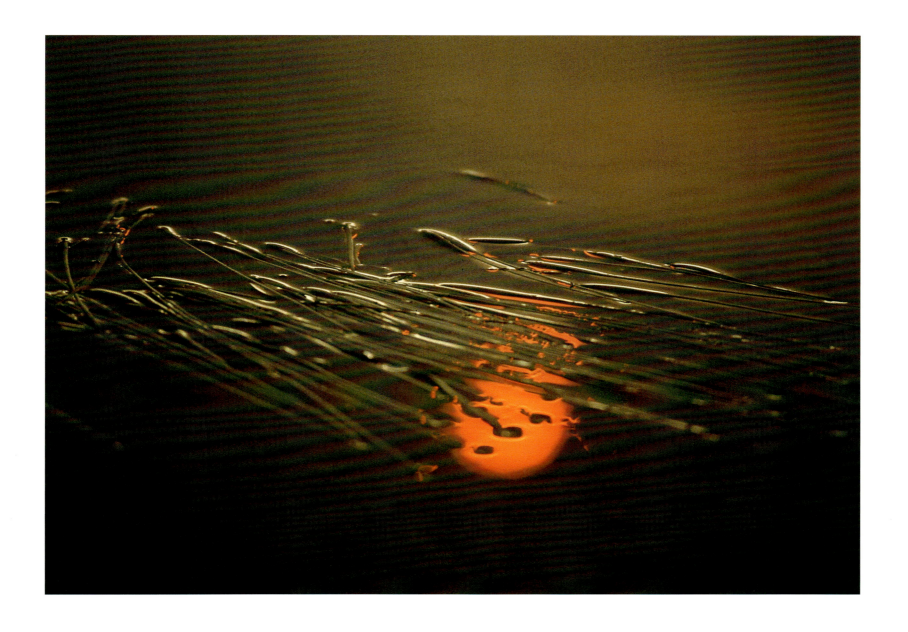

Red bearberries.

A tiny leaf-hopper sits atop a mushroom.

A mushroom enfolds an alder catkin.

Facing page: A bull moose in his prime.

Above: Moose spend a large amount of time feeding on aquatic plants. Some even venture into deep water and dive for plants on the bottom.

Eastern Slopes

The weather is wet and overcast. A cold wind sweeps mist along the high land above the Tuchodi River. Our friend Tom Perry has been shooting video footage, but I haven't seen him for some time. I call to my partner Marce Fofonoff at the back of the pack string, "Have you seen Tom?" "Not for a while . . . " Night is coming on and we can't wait.

An hour later we make a hasty camp in the valley, call, and fire off the rifle, but silence is the only answer. Quickly gathering a few supplies and leaving Marce to take care of camp and the pack string, journalist Larry Pynn and I head back up the trail in the gathering dusk, stopping only briefly to check for signs of Tom. Halfway up the mountain, the tracks of a massive grizzly blot our horses' prints, made just two hours before. Could this explain Tom's disappearance?

The crystal waters of Henry Creek, Northern Rocky Mountains Provincial Park, indicate that no glaciers are melting upstream.

A herd of elk grazes the green hillsides of the Tuchodi Valley.

For the past 10 days, we have been following the flanks of the Rockies south from Stone Mountain Park along the High Trail corridor. Our 1995 expedition has been a series of long hard climbs over high alpine passes, then knee-jarring plunges into the next valley bottom of streams like the Tetsa, Henry and Chisca. If the first North Americans followed an ice free corridor down the Rockies to colonize the continent, this is the route they would have taken.

Low snowpacks and hospitable terrain on the broadly rounded mountains of the Rockies' eastern foothills create rich wildlife wintering grounds. On our expedition through Northern Rocky Mountains Park, we have seen countless elk, many caribou and moose, as well as mountain sheep and goats. This 665,700-hectare (1.64 million acre) park is larger than many European countries. Like all Class A parks in B.C., it is off-limits to road building and industrial activity.

As we travel south, range after range of mountains spread before us. To the north, south and west of the park lie several Special Management Zones where forestry, mining and natural gas exploration is allowed. Managing these activities, particularly road construction and reclamation, in a way that maintains wilderness and wildlife here in the sensitive eastern slopes will be a major challenge. Elsewhere, examples abound of exploration roads and

66

"... a cold wind sweeping the mist along the high mountainsides above the Tuchodi River..." Tom Perry and Marce Fofonoff on the trail.

development activity which have destroyed the natural values of the wilderness. Here, things must be done differently.

But tonight, our concerns are more immediate. We work back up the mountain in search of Tom but by the time we reach the alpine, we cannot make out the elk that grunts from the buckbrush. Although we find one boot track in the mud, it is soon too dark to see anything more. We turn and lead our saddle horses back down a steep hogsback, slipping and sliding on the slick grass. In the valley, the eerie howls of a wolf pack echo in the crisp cool night, as clouds slide across a three quarter moon.

At first light we saddle up and ride down river to Ross Peck's outfitting camp. "Did you lose something?" greets us as we ride into the clearing. "I think we've got something of yours!"

Unable to pick up our trail through the thick willows on the mountainside, Tom built a small fire under a spruce tree, then made his way to Peck's at first light. It was an impressive display of cool headedness and bushcraft in a tough situation.

Top left: Frequent trail companion Andy Kadziolka grits his teeth and hangs on in a deep crossing of the Muskwa River while Reed Radley and Marce Fofonoff wait to cross.

Bottom: Packing camp on a wet and windy morning. The horses are saddled, the fire is out, and the tarp is ready to come down before we hit the trail.

Below: The author's nephew, Dylan Sawchuk, adjusts a feed basket while horses jostle for position in the string.

On our annual summer expedition we spend six to 10 weeks on the trail, exploring new routes through the mountains. Fresh trail participants fly in, usually to a convenient lake along our route. Here we do a change in July 2003, at East Tuchodi Lake, with aircraft flown by Liard Air out of Muncho Lake.

These pages: East Tuchodi Lake.

Overleaf pages 72 and 73: The Neves Creek valley and the Neves Designated Access Route, originally an oil and gas exploration road. Note the differing vegetation on either side of the road in the far left centre of the photograph, an example of an unanticipated result likely related to a change in groundwater flows.

Reflecting pool and Tetsa Lake.

Pack string, seen through an ice cave in a melting snowfield brought down by a winter avalanche in the Tuchodi valley.

Frost and gravity produce a striking landscape above Tetsa Lake. (Photo of Tetsa Lake on page 74 was taken from the low ridge at the far end of the lake.)

Natural weathering produces brilliant colours in shale near Henry Creek.

Lichen on rock near the Besa River.

Top left and right: Lichen patterns on rock.	Bottom: Close-up of rusty shale, Henry Creek.

Frost-covered willow, Besa River.

Hoodoos in the Wokkpash valley.

Upper Sikanni Falls, Sikanni River, and Mount Bertha. This area is designated as a Special Management Zone, where natural gas exploration is allowed. An unsuccessful natural gas well was drilled a few kilometers from this spot, and future gas drilling is likely. This is an example of a landscape where extra care and sensitive techniques are required.

Left: A herd of cow and calf caribou, upper Macdonald Creek.

Below: A caribou track shows widely spreading dew claws, an adaptation for travel in snow, mud, moss and other soft surfaces.

Falls Creek, Tuchodi River valley.

Small falls, Tetsa River valley.

Peace – Finlay

Once more, we check the compass, and scour the map. But it is no use. There is no view to be had from the thick timber of the McCook River valley, and we can see little of the distant mountaintops. The year is 1996 and we are one week's travel out of Fort Ware. We can tell where north is, but that's all! Some might see it as a technical distinction, but we're not LOST. We can always get back to Fox Lake and down the Rocky Mountain Trench to the Fort.

What a trip that would be! Both riders and horses are showing the wear from miles of windfall, bugs, bush and seemingly endless quaking bogs. The 32-hour barge trip up Williston Lake to Ingenika, then the early morning trip north in a careening stock truck on narrow logging roads to Fort Ware, and the rough trip that followed up the Davie Trail and the Rocky Mountain Trench were rigorous enough.

A melting glacier left this boulder perched high above the headwaters of the Akie River.

"... Marce, George Smith, Reed Radley and I find ourselves high on the side of a mountain, above the headwaters of the McCook River tracking a rough caribou trail over rocks and avalanche debris."

After turning east at Fox Lake, the trip deteriorated even further into the endurance marathon we'd just come through.

Still, we are headed north, or so we think, for Driftpile Creek and the Gataga River. Three days after leaving Fox Lake, Marce, George Smith, Reed Radley and I find ourselves high on the side of a mountain, above the headwaters of the McCook River tracking a rough caribou trail over rocks and avalanche debris.

Then, a choice. The valley below forks, one side curving east around the end of our mountain, the other fork turning northwest. A quick traverse on foot brings us out above a deep valley to the east – and there below, water sparkles. To our surprise, it is the South Gataga Lakes – we are miles east of where we intended to be!

We head up the northwest valley, already late for our bush plane rendezvous, and two days later find ourselves stumbling through timber approaching our destination cabin. We push on into the night through a cold, soaking rain. As the darkness deepens, only Reed's small flashlight allows us to locate the trail as it traverses from bog to bog across the valley.

It is a tough lesson in bush travel. Leaving Fox Lake, we had changed our plans at the last minute and headed east on an untried route. We had no

"Both riders and horses are showing the wear . . ." The end of a long day in the Rocky Mountain Trench.

detailed maps of the new area we were heading into and the slopes of the Rocky Mountain Trench are no place for a pleasure ride. The mountains on either side are rugged, and each passing cloud drops moisture on the western upslope. As a result, thick timber cloaks the valleys and sidehills. The rivers run high and deep, the Ospika, Akie, Kwadacha, Warneford and McCook from the east, with the powerful Finlay, joined by the Obo, Spinel and Thudaka coursing down from the west.

The Fox and Obo Special Management Zones are open to industrial exploitation, including forestry, and the land use plan allows permanent mainline roads to be built here in the future. This is the only place where the construction of permanent roads is allowed in the Muskwa-Kechika.

It will be a significant challenge to carry out forestry here in a way that respects the intent of the Muskwa-Kechika Management Area Act, the land use plan, and the wishes of First Nations. The character of this rugged land will change forever with the coming of the roads. A lot of work must be done to address this issue, much of it by First Nations who are working to define how logging will be carried out here in the future.

Facing page: Caribou tracks dot the bottom of an alpine tarn, near the Rocky Mountain divide, at the head of the Akie River.

Top left: The Fox River contains valuable low elevation habitat and timber resources. It is also an area heavily used by First Nations now and in the past. This site at Nine-mile (north of Fort Ware) is on the Davie Trail.

Top right: An outfitter's camp looks out over Fox Lake in the Rocky Mountain Trench.

Bottom: Facing a tricky crossing on the Akie. Large boulders, deep water and a fast current all spell danger.

Facing page: The setting sun lights a mountain on the Akie River.

Above: The rushing waters of the upper Akie River.

The upper Akie River.

Left: Burnt timber on the Akie River.

Below: Arnicas bring new life to a recently burnt forest floor.

An arm of the Lloyd George Icefield cascades down to icebound Hayworth Lake.

Summer on the Rocky Mountain divide between the Akie and Prophet rivers, not far from Hayworth Lake.

Facing page: Fleabane and monkshood in a subalpine meadow.

Above: Larkspur in a montane meadow.

Kechika-Liard

The day is hot and dry and the Frog is running deep and wide, fed by melting snows upstream. The icy water rises neck deep on the saddle horses as we rein them into the current. Suddenly, a shout – "Wayne, the foals!"

A long hard month of travel, in the summer of 1999, from Dease Lake east through the Cassiars to Terminus Mountain, the northernmost peak of the Rockies, has brought us to the Frog River. The two valiant foals have endured rocks and mud, heat, bugs, quaking bogs, and long stretches of wilderness devoid of trails, as we skirt the "pole of inaccessibility," over 100 km (60 mi.) from the nearest road. This is as remote as it is possible to be in the interior of the province. We have crossed the Turnagain, Tucho, and Denatiah rivers without incident, but not the Frog.

Early fall on the Toad River.

"The two valiant foals have endured rocks and mud, heat, bugs, quaking bogs, and long stretches of wilderness devoid of trails . . ."

Nostrils flaring and snorting water, the foals struggle against the current, unable to break the grip of the river. It is dragging them slowly downstream into a blind channel, choked from bank to bank with logs.

The water deepens quickly, both shores too steep to climb. To enter would mean being trapped in deep water, unable to swim free, with the frothy teeth of the logjam bared menacingly below. Suddenly, I sight a small ramp of sand, just above the jam. A chance! With water rising to my chest I urge my saddlehorse downstream. As his hooves leave the bottom he surges toward the foals. They turn to follow with desperate eagerness in their terrified eyes. In just a moment more, we clamber up the steep narrow sandbank and into the trees beyond. Their panic gone with the first firm foothold, the foals push and prance, eager to rejoin their mares. A close call!

The next day we come to the Kechika River, the largest undeveloped watershed in the province at 2.2 million ha (5.44 million acres). This river flows north along the Rocky Mountain Trench to meet the mighty Liard River in the vast lowlands of the Liard Basin, their combined force sufficient to break through the Rocky Mountains at the northern end of the Muskwa-Kechika. After crossing the Kechika, we make our way south along the mountains and across the Gataga River. Then we turn north again over the Rocky

". . . we make our way south along the mountains . . ." On the upper Through Creek, located in the Braid Special: Wildland RMZ, west of the Gataga River. The rounded mountains in the background contain staked lead zinc deposits.

Mountain divide at Ram Lakes and head down the Toad River to meet the Alaska Highway at Mile 442, in Muncho Lake Park. This journey will take us through some of the wildest country in North America. In one valley we do not find a single axe cut, fire pit or other sign of humans. For over a month, we meet no one on the trail, and there are no signs of people or horses from this year. We seem to be the only humans in a vast and thriving wilderness!

In the mountains west of the Gataga, we pass huge red scars on the mountainsides, natural "kill zones" advertising lead zinc deposits. The land use plans (to which the mining sector did not agree) and the Muskwa-Kechika Management Area Act recognize that mining may exploit such deposits in the future, if wilderness, wildlife and habitat can be maintained. This could be a tall order in these pristine and trackless mountains. It is an example of the delicate balance inherent in the Muskwa-Kechika, for all Resource Management Zones outside of parks are open for sub-surface resource exploitation, and most are open for forestry. Notable exceptions are the Special: Wildland RMZs, located in the western areas of the Muskwa-Kechika. Because of relatively low timber values, high wilderness and wildlife values, and expensive road building costs, these are off limits to commercial timber harvesting.

Facing page: Pack string on the upper Gataga, just below the Rocky Mountain divide.

Above: Big Dan is our biggest packhorse and always gets the heaviest load. As a result, he is also the first to go down in a swamp. A veteran, he waits patiently while Marce unpacks him and the signal is given to "OK, get up!" On his nose he wears a "feed basket," (actually an ANTI-feed basket) designed to eliminate feeding and the resulting trouble on the trail.

Marce and a foal on an early fall day on Sheep Creek, off the Gataga River.

Facing page: Dwarf or shrub birch and red bearberry light up the Ram Lakes valley, on the Rocky Mountain divide.

Below: Red bearberry leaves glow neon in the fall.

The Liard Hotsprings emit clouds of mist on a cool October morning.

The Alaska Highway is an adventure road. 200 km (120 mi.) lie within the Muskwa-Kechika, and here wildlife abounds.

Top: A black bear tanks up on grass just before heading off to hibernate for the winter. How soon? First Nations say: "The leaves will cover him in his den."

Bottom left: The Muskwa-Kechika is home to herds of free-ranging bison. These animals have been re-introduced and are colonizing their former ranges.

Bottom right: A bull moose heads across the highway at Muncho Lake.

Facing page: The Alaska Highway near Toad River in early fall.

Facing page: The author's uncle, Norman Sawchuk, leads the way down a long, cold trail back to camp on the upper Driftpile Creek.

Below: A sudden late September snow squall on the Driftpile mountains dusts our saddle horses while we take cover.

Left: What made these tracks? They just end, out there on the snow-covered ice. Or maybe they begin? The landing tracks of a flying squirrel point to a take-off from the tall trees on the background ridge.

Below: The tracks of a moose cross a frozen lake in the deep snows of March.

Previous pages 120 and 121: Mayfield Lakes, on the Gataga River, on a glittering morning in March.

Greater scaup flash across a northern lake.

Moose Lake, on the Toad River.

Left: A raft floats by thick deposits of glacial clay on the Gataga River.

Below: Mountain goats obtain vital minerals using the glacial clays as a lick.

Moose Lake, on the Toad River.

A single wolf track on the Gataga River. How did it get there?

Two small waterfalls, just off the Alaska Highway.

the Future

High on the headwaters of a remote river, a hundred years from now, a mother grizzly watches her cubs frolic in a sunny alpine meadow next to a stream of cold sparkling water. A herd of caribou dot the skyline far above and a bull elk bugles from the timberline. A pair of wolves pause to watch a train of packhorses cross the valley far below, while above, a golden eagle soars. Farther east, an unseen subterranean well head quietly pumps natural gas, and a herd of mountain sheep feed on a reclaimed mine site, indistinguishable from the natural landscape around it. On a nearby river, a First Nations group camps, hunts moose and gathers medicines, as they have always done.

All this and more will happen in the Muskwa-Kechika – if the vision of the land use plans is realized. The alternative is not pleasant to contemplate – viewscapes scarred and damaged by industrial activity, wildlife populations reduced to remnants, wilderness recreation a thing of the past and traditional lifestyles only a memory. Either of these future scenarios is possible.

Ensuring that this priceless legacy exists for future generations will take everyone's best efforts. To maintain the fragile values that exist in this outstanding land, each user, whether government, industrialist or recreationalist, must operate to the highest standards possible. Permanent and all-season roads must not be used in the search for natural gas. Instead, ice roads and heli-portable drilling technology will create as little impact as possible. Mining activity must be designed to have minimal impact to wildlife and ecosystems while operating, and must leave no visible scars after reclamation. Forestry activity must be planned to

The author's son Dan paddles the golden waters of Mayfield Lake.

appear natural, and must remove all roads and access between passes or entries, which should be limited to as few as possible.

Forestry in a wilderness landscape is a challenging concept, and comprehensive pre-planning will be required before an acceptable forest harvesting strategy can be developed.

At present, there are few limits on commercial and non-commercial recreation in the Muskwa-Kechika. An exception is the Muskwa-Kechika Access Management Area, which designates routes that allow motorized all terrain vehicle access. In the future, it may become necessary to manage additional recreational activities, should they increase to a level that damages conservation values or the recreational experiences of other users.

It will be crucial that the zones and management objectives that have been put in place continue to be upheld. For instance, the agreements reached at the planning tables were built on the understanding that no roads would be constructed in the provincial parks. To change this would destabilize the land use agreements of northeastern B.C.

Can we now say that the Muskwa-Kechika is a success? The truth is: it's too early to tell.

Since the completion of the land use plans, much has been accomplished. Legislation is now in place, the Muskwa-Kechika Advisory Board is up and running, and the Muskwa-Kechika Fund is regularly supporting worthwhile projects. On the operational side, the Chicken Creek natural gas exploration project utilized innovative snow fill technology to build a temporary road and two wellsite locations, creating minimum impact in a very sensitive mountain valley.

But, as of the dawn of 2004, there have been some disturbing developments.

After the Chicken Creek project, two subsequent natural gas projects elsewhere in the Muskwa-Kechika used much more damaging conventional techniques, including cut and fill wellsite construction methods that created a much greater level of damage to soils, vegetation, visual quality and waterflow patterns.

Next, a road corridor has been allowed through the Graham-Laurier Park, inside the Muskwa-Kechika, against the recommendations of the approved Fort St. John Land and Resource Management Plan.

And, recent changes have weakened the Muskwa-Kechika itself. Guaranteed funding for the Muskwa-Kechika Fund has been reduced by two-thirds, the critical "joint sign-off" mechanism ensuring interagency cooperation has been eliminated, staffing for the Muskwa-Kechika and most land agencies has been diminished, support for many First Nations' cultural and

economic interests has been reduced and the advisory board has been directed to focus funds on completing oil and gas planning before adequate conservation science information is in place.

On the plus side, the present provincial government has indicated ongoing support for the Muskwa-Kechika Management Area, the board and the fund. Work is currently being done by board members, First Nations, sectoral interests (including industry) and government to ensure that the Muskwa-Kechika Management Area model does indeed thrive and evolve. There is now recognition that the original legislation was visionary but incomplete, and options are being proposed to design effective and cooperative governance for both the Muskwa-Kechika board and relevant government ministries. Better ways to respect and include aboriginal values and rights are being pursued. A new funding mechanism is being examined to facilitate a more effective and independent board.

It appears the Muskwa-Kechika is at a critical point in its history. If we meet the challenges facing the Muskwa-Kechika, we will have created a model that is the envy of the world – a radical new approach to the pressures of ever-increasing rates of resource extraction as it encroaches on the last few remnants of wild nature. This model can be applied wherever wilderness and wildlife face similar challenges the world over. We owe it to future generations to do everything in our power to make sure it does not fail.

By working together, I believe we will make this incredible experiment a success, enjoy a strong, vibrant and sustainable economy and keep the wild heart of Canada's Northern Rockies beating strong forever.

Facing page and above, left to right:

Habitat fragmentation from a single snowmobile track. A caribou encountering the track refuses to cross. What would be the results of multiple snowmobile tracks? Perhaps, over time, a degrading of habitat value for this vulnerable species.

Another effect of access. A caribou bull narrowly escapes an encounter with a transport truck on the Alaska Highway. Many are not so lucky.

Damaging road construction practices on an oil and gas exploration road on the north end of Butler Ridge, just south of the Muskwa-Kechika. The effects of this road will continue to be visible a century from now. Roads of this kind are no longer allowed in the Muskwa-Kechika.

An innovative oil and gas exploration project in the Muskwa-Kechika. The Chicken Creek project used artificial snow to create a base for a winter road and two temporary shale wellsites. These wells were drilled in an important wildlife wintering area without any disturbance of the original ground surface.

The Chicken Creek wellsite and road location as they appeared the season after wellsite and road removal. The original vegetation is greening up on the wellsite location, (which remained in place for two winter seasons) while the road location has regained its original appearance and cannot be seen in this photograph.

White with glacial flour, the upper Gataga River races down from the Rocky Mountain divide.

*"It is my fervent hope
that these photographs will help keep the Muskwa-Kechika
wild and free, forever."*

PHOTOGRAPHER'S NOTES

Inside, the cabin glows with warmth. Outside, the air is crisp and cold. A thin column of smoke rises straight into the night, outlined in the bright light of a moon almost full behind high misty cloud. To the west across the valley, mountain peaks lie still and white, half obscured by a wash of ice crystals hanging in the winter air.

It seems the whole world must be quiet tonight. Of course, beyond this wilderness, the din of human activity carries on, but here, it is a privilege to hear nothing but the deep and profound sound of silence.

Inspired once again by the surrounding magnificence, I turn back to the cabin. Images and possibilities fill my mind. I pull off mitts, reach for my cameras, and prepare to return to the clear, cold night.

For me, the act of taking the picture is the most enjoyable part of photography: composing the shot, finding the angle that has the best balance and the best flow, capturing the action or the mood. Creative impulses take over, and minutes or hours go by in a flash. Only later, looking over the finished images, do I fully realize and appreciate what I have captured.

I use two systems, a 35 mm Minolta and a 645 Pentax, with a selection of lenses for each. Since we are often out on the trail for months at a time, with little possibility of resupply, it is important to bring along spares and replacements, a lens brush or two and extra batteries for each type of camera.

When heading out for an expedition, I take along two Minolta 35 mm bodies: an older Maxxum 7000 and a newer Maxxum 800si. The 7000 doesn't have as many useful features, such as auto bracketing, and the auto focus is slower than the 800si, but it is a very reliable camera and makes an excellent back-up. The spare camera body has frequently prevented disaster. During the day, I carry the 800si with a 24 to 105 mm zoom lens in my saddle bag, along with lens brush and cloth, spare battery and lots of film.

I use Fuji Velvia slide film almost exclusively. Although slow at ISO 50, it provides excellent grain and great saturation of blues and greens, a benefit for many outdoor subjects. I do however, find that Velvia has a limited contrast range: a partly shaded subject in bright sunlight will usually be lost with overblown highlights or underexposed shadows. For a broader contrast range or where extra speed is required, such as shooting from a plane, I use Fuji Provia 100 or occasionally a faster speed. I seldom use an ISO higher than 200, in order to maintain the finest grain possible.

On a long wilderness trip, I ration film to one roll of 36 per day plus a half dozen extra rolls for special occasions. Of course, no matter how much film I bring, it is never enough!

The 24 to 105 mm zoom is a great focal length range to have quickly at hand, perfect for candid shots of people or to capture the quickly shifting light of an outdoor scene. I also carry a macro lens for extreme

A long exposure creates star trails, several small electronic flashes light the cabin, and a double exposure places the moon in the photo, in this composite image created on a single transparency.

Sun from behind, view to the front. What to do? Shoot! The photographer and his equipment become part of the image.

close-ups, and I enjoy the way a 20 mm wide angle squeezes that extra bit of landscape into the frame. I recently acquired a Tamron AF 300 mm 2.8 telephoto – a wonderfully sharp lens that has meant a quantum leap in my ability to photograph wildlife. It's a bit heavy, and relatively expensive, but worth every ounce and cent. I wish I had made the leap years ago!

Even though I still rely heavily on the 35 mm format, I have for years found it frustrating. No matter how careful I was, taking every precaution with tripod, cable release and fine grained film, somehow my shots never seemed quite crisp enough when blown up to poster size. Finally, I understood that this problem is inherent to the small size of the 35 mm format. Consequently, I upgraded to a 645 Pentax system which creates an image about three times larger than a 35 mm. It has opened up a world of detail and the capacity for enlarging has multiplied by three. This camera is heavy compared to the 35 mm system, so I use a tripod for almost every shot. My favorite lens with this system is a 35 mm wide angle, equivalent to a 21 mm lens in a 35 mm system. It is fantastic for those great depth of focus landscapes, rich in detail from foreground to background.

With both systems, I use polarizing filters to remove glare and saturate color, and to enhance the whiteness of clouds against the deep blue sky, but I don't use coloured filters. A graduated gray filter, though, is invaluable when the contrast range exceeds that of the film – a sunlit

Shadows reveal the missing packhorses in an image created on the Rocky Mountain divide near Tuchodi Lakes. My good saddlehorse Bonus adds to the image by gazing into the shot.

mountain with a shadowed foreground, or a meadow in the foreground backed by a brightly lit glacier. The graduated gray filter holds back the areas that are too bright, rendering a balanced overall exposure. Without this filter, it would not be possible to take these difficult pictures successfully.

I like to work with what's before me, without posing the subject or arranging objects. If I meddle with the shot, the result never looks natural, at least not to me. This is where my philosophies of photography and life overlap: no matter how I try, I just can't seem to do better than nature. Except for the contrast on two or three reproductions, the images in this book have not been digitally enhanced – they appear as they were shot. Nor do I shoot captive or caged wildlife. All of the animals in these photographs are free and wild, and all were photographed within or close to the Muskwa-Kechika itself. All but two of the remaining images (page 106, Letain Lake just west of the M-K boundary, and page 137, left, Butler Ridge) were shot within the Muskwa-Kechika.

In spite of the deep silence that rests on this land, it is not empty. Uncountable creatures live out their lives here, part of an intricate and ageless web, still intact, healthy and thriving. The people, plants and animals, rivers and rocks, are all part of this living wonder called the Muskwa-Kechika. It is my fervent hope that these photographs will help keep the Muskwa-Kechika wild and free, forever.

In much of the backcountry of the Muskwa-Kechika, the moose come out any time of day, unconcerned and undisturbed by man. This little bull moose with his mother represents hope – the hope that they and others like them will have the opportunity to live as they always have, in a Muskwa-Kechika that remains unimpaired forever. Let's hope, and work to make it so.